INTO THE ARENA: EMPERORS & GLADIATORS

Written by Ben Hubbard

Illustrated by Laszlo Veres and Norbert Sipos

CONTENTS

Collins

INTRODUCTION

Imagine joining a crowd of thousands to watch gladiators fight to the death in a sandy **arena** before you. Imagine sitting in a vast **amphitheatre** for daylong spectacles that included animal hunts, animal battles and public executions. Imagine these events being so popular that they ran for days, or even weeks at a time. These were Rome's gladiatorial games.

The people at the centre of these games were the emperors and the gladiators. The gladiators were mostly prisoners of war, or enslaved people who had escaped, who were forced to fight. After swearing an **oath**, gladiators were trained to fight in an amphitheatre before thousands of spectators.

The emperor views the gladiators from his imperial box.

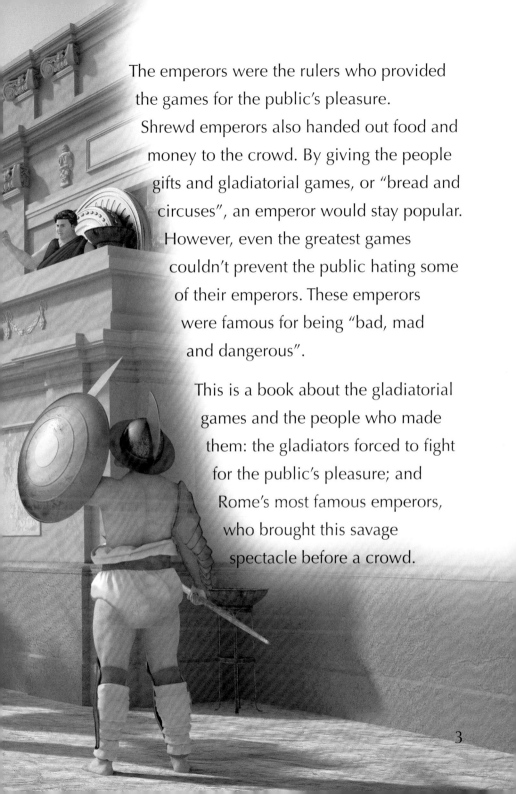

The emperors were the rulers who provided the games for the public's pleasure.

Shrewd emperors also handed out food and money to the crowd. By giving the people gifts and gladiatorial games, or "bread and circuses", an emperor would stay popular. However, even the greatest games couldn't prevent the public hating some of their emperors. These emperors were famous for being "bad, mad and dangerous".

This is a book about the gladiatorial games and the people who made them: the gladiators forced to fight for the public's pleasure; and Rome's most famous emperors, who brought this savage spectacle before a crowd.

1 A DAY AT THE GAMES

There would be a great buzz in the air in the days before the gladiatorial games. Advertisements for the games would be painted on city walls, providing all the details. They would announce which gladiators were fighting, the comforts provided to spectators, and how long the games would last.

gladiators in the forum

A day before the games began, the gladiators would be
paraded in the city's public square, known as a forum.
This introduced excited spectators to the men who
would fight for their entertainment. After the parade,
the gladiators would be thrown a banquet, with rich,
exotic food. Smart gladiators wouldn't eat food so different
from their daily porridge. This could cause stomach upsets
in the amphitheatre the next day. Instead, they used
the occasion to say goodbye to loved ones and make their
funeral arrangements.

On the bill

Advertisements for the games
would be painted by
poster artists. They would list
the events, such as animal hunts
and public executions, as well
as comforts for the spectators
that could include sun awnings
and sprayed, perfumed water.
The names and types of gladiators
would also appear. Most gladiators
took a stage name, such as
"Flamma" (the flame).

THE MORNING HUNTS

On the morning of the games, throngs of people would head towards the amphitheatre. As they entered, these spectators would buy snacks, rent cushions for comfort, and share gossip with other spectators. Then, they would find their seats.

The chatter from the crowd would mingle with sinister sounds from below the sandy arena floor. Here, trumpeting elephants, growling lions and howling wolves would pace their cages. When two cages released their animals into the arena, the morning's entertainment had begun. The crowd loved unexpected pairings, such as a bull against a bear, or a tiger against a lion. Only one animal would leave the arena alive.

After the animal fights, sets such as trees and bushes would emerge through trapdoors in the arena floor. Then, animals such as ostriches, deer, panthers, bears and lions would be let loose into this "wildlife set". These animals were then hunted down with arrows and spears. Afterwards, their carcasses would be dragged away and fresh sand sprinkled over the blood. Perfumed water was often sprayed from jets over the crowd, to disguise the smell. The morning's entertainment was over.

AFTERNOON GLADIATORS

Lunchtime at the games would be set aside for the executions of condemned criminals and enemies of Rome. Not everyone enjoyed watching the executions. Many used the opportunity to leave the amphitheatre to stretch their legs, use the public toilets outside, or eat in one of the nearby bars.

After the bodies of the executed were removed and fresh sand laid down, returning spectators would again find their seats in the early-afternoon sun. Now, the amphitheatre would be sizzling with excitement for the crowd's favourite event: the gladiator fights.

A hush would fall across the crowd, as the opening ceremony began. Trumpets sounded as a procession of musicians, men carrying weapons, the organisers in togas and the gladiators entered the arena. The gladiators would stretch, flex and show off their muscles. Then they would depart from the arena, as the sharpness of the weapons was checked. Sometimes, the Roman emperor himself entered to do this.

During the opening ceremony, gladiators would sometimes warm up with wooden practice weaponry.

Gladiator music

Musicians on trumpets, horns and tubas would play along to a gladiator fight, making the music soft, loud, or climactic to suit the action.

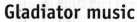

9

BATTLE BEGINS

Trumpets would sound as the first two gladiators and the referee entered the arena. Little is known today about the rules of combat. However, the ancient crowd certainly understood them. As with modern football, spectators would make their feelings clear by shouting, jeering and cheering throughout every moment of a fight.

Gladiators were expected to fight without fear and die with honour, if their time was up.

For the gladiators, their many hours of training with wooden swords would suddenly become a matter of life or death. They would use their swords to lunge and thrust, although their blades would rarely cross. Instead, they would use their shields to stop blows, hit their opponent, or knock the sword from their hand. Meanwhile, both gladiators would scan each other's bodies for a vulnerable part to cut or thrust their blade into.

Taking breaks

There were no rounds in a gladiator contest and the combat would go on until one was declared the winner. A fight could be as short as two minutes, but was typically between ten and 15 minutes long. In longer contests, the referee would call for a break. Assistants would then massage the gladiators' sore muscles and serve them drinks.

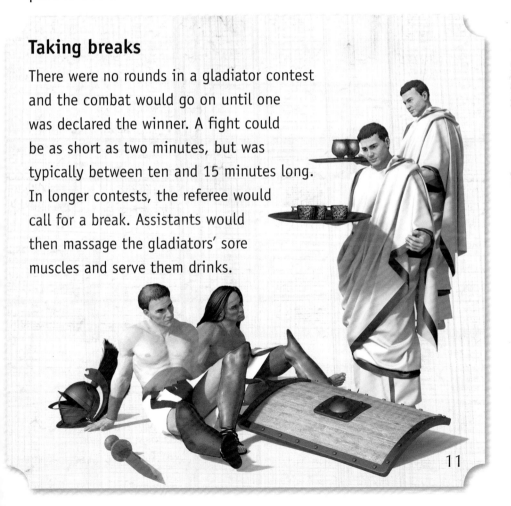

FIGHT TILL THE END

Many gladiator fights ended in death. Others ended
when one was too exhausted or injured to continue.
Then, the defeated gladiator would throw down his
sword, or raise his index finger to **submit**. His opponent
would then look to the emperor for further instruction.
The emperor would look to the crowd. If the spectators
"turned their thumbs" to indicate the gladiator should live,
the emperor might let the gladiator leave the arena alive.
If not, the gladiator was expected to wrap his arms and legs
around his opponent to receive a death blow between his
shoulder blades.

The victorious gladiator would then approach the imperial box to receive applause and his purse of coins. He would get to fight another day.

All emperors wanted spectators to leave the games satisfied, but especially those emperors who were worried about being disliked. Some would therefore hand out grain, meat, money, or other gifts. Then, in the late afternoon, the crowd would walk back through the streets to their homes. There would be more games tomorrow, or even the next. Emperor Trajan's 107 CE games ran for 123 days in a row and featured 10,000 gladiators.

Refusing to fight

Sometimes gladiators refused to fight. When this happened, armed assistants would force them into action.

2 THE ORIGIN OF THE GAMES

The first gladiator fights weren't performed in an amphitheatre in front of a crowd. Instead, they began at the funerals of Roman **aristocrats** in the 3rd century BCE. Here, armed men would fight to the death to honour the dead.

A funeral in ancient Rome was called a *munus*. A *munus* was an important event because it was a chance for Rome's richest families to show off their wealth and power to those attending. The first recorded Roman *munus* was in 264 BCE, to honour aristocrat Junius Brutus Pera. At the *munus*, three pairs of gladiators fought in the city's forum. As time went on, a *munus* became a far grander event. In 183 BCE, a *munus* for aristocrat Publius Licinius lasted for three days and featured 60 pairs of gladiators. Free meat was given out to spectators afterwards. Later, it was expected that every *munus* would be a spectacular event followed by a banquet.

a *munus* during the Roman Republic

14

The forum

A square in the middle of a city, the forum was the centre of ancient Roman life. Public announcements, processions, markets and gladiator fights would all be held in the forum.

the forum in ancient Rome

the forum in modern times

PUBLIC GAMES

THE LUDI

In early Rome, a *munus* was a privately-funded event.
But public games were also held. Called *ludi*, these were
often held to celebrate a Roman victory in war.
By the 2nd century BCE, the Roman army had
conquered many territories outside of its Italian borders.
Through a policy of conquest, it would grow into the most
successful civilisation of the ancient world.

CIRCUS MAXIMUS

Ludi held at Rome's Circus Maximus were a crowd favourite.
A long, U-shaped arena, the circus could seat 150,000
spectators and was purpose-built to hold chariot races.
Romans both rich and poor alike loved the races.
They were also fiercely loyal to one of the four chariot teams,
who wore uniforms of red, white, blue or green.

a mosaic of a chariot race

Chariot races were fast, furious events, where a charioteer drove a team of two or four horses for seven laps of the circus. To help them win, charioteers would try and cause accidents among their opponents. As a result, there were many accidents and even deaths.

Circus Maximus

Roman circuses weren't like the "Big Top" circuses that we know today. Instead, they were open-air entertainment venues where *ludi* were held. This is how Rome's Circus Maximus looks now.

ENTER THE ANIMALS

In the 2nd century, *ludi* at the Circus Maximus took a new twist with the introduction of animals. Wild animals from newly-conquered Roman territories were of great interest to *ludi* spectators. Most had never seen exotic creatures such as elephants, lions and camels before.

To begin with, animals were simply paraded in front of the spectators at the circus. However, after being transported long distances across land and sea, many animals were too exhausted or hungry to stand. Others, angry at being locked up, would try to attack the audience.

After a while, it was decided that parading animals wasn't enough. Instead, they would be hunted and killed. During these animal hunts, sets of trees, logs and bushes would be placed in the Circus Maximus. The animals would be released from their cages. Hunters on horseback would then chase them down.

Roman Republic

The Roman civilisation was originally founded in 753 BCE, in Rome, Italy. Over time, it covered the country of modern-day Italy. From 509 BCE, Rome was a **republic**: a **democracy** controlled by a **Senate**, rather than an emperor. A Roman emperor was a male who was born to rule. The Roman Republic conquered large territories outside its Italian borders. During times of war and danger, senators could elect a **dictator** to rule for a short period.

Under the emperors, Rome became the largest **empire** in the ancient world. At its peak, Rome stretched over five million square kilometres and ruled over 60 million people. In the late 3rd century CE, Rome was divided into the Eastern Roman Empire and Western Roman Empire.

CAESAR'S GAMES

Julius Caesar was a famous Roman general and senator who craved power. He gained great popularity by holding large, lavish *munera* (plural for *munus*) and *ludi*. In doing so, he created the **blueprint** for the gladiatorial games.

Caesar knew the people of Rome could easily rebel and overthrow an unpopular leader. The key to power was therefore pleasing the people. And nothing pleased the Roman people more than a good show. Caesar gave them this with an elaborate *ludi* at the Circus Maximus. He borrowed money to import 400 lions to be hunted down at this event. Next, Caesar held a *munus* for his father, even though he had died 20 years earlier. At the *munus*, over 300 gladiators fought to the death. The event was considered a great success.

Who was Caesar?

Born in 100 BCE to a rich Roman family, Julius Caesar went into politics at a young age. In 59 BCE, he was elected to **Consul**, the highest position in the Roman Republic. As a general and governor, Caesar conquered all of Gaul (modern-day France) before entering into a **civil war** with another general, Pompey. After defeating Pompey, the Senate elected Caesar as dictator as Rome was still considered at threat. In theory, the title granted Caesar special powers for a temporary period.

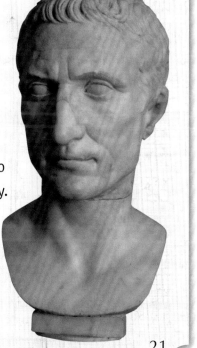

BREAD AND CIRCUSES

After being made dictator, Caesar began behaving
like an all-powerful emperor. He built a new forum in
Rome and announced a *munus* would be held for his
deceased daughter, Julia. He ordered new gladiators be
trained specially for this *munus* and gifts be prepared for
the crowd.

After the *munus* for Julia, Caesar organised even
bigger gladiatorial games. He also gave grain, olive
oil and 400 *sestertii* (Roman money) to each citizen
of Rome. This was an expensive gift. It was also
a clever move. Caesar's "bread and circuses" would
ensure he stayed popular. Caesar wasn't so popular among
the senators of Rome, however.

By 44 BCE, some Roman senators believed Caesar had
become a **tyrant** who thought of himself as an emperor.
On 15th March, several senators stabbed Caesar to death
outside the Senate building. The Roman people were
horrified when they found out. They loved Julius Caesar and
called for his killers to be executed. Rome was in peril.

NEW CAESAR

After Caesar's murder,
Rome once again fell
into civil war. The victor
of this war was Caesar's
heir, Octavian. After punishing
Caesar's killers, Octavian changed
his name to Augustus and gave himself
the title "First Citizen". This made him
Rome's first emperor in all but name.
The Senate would continue, but no
longer had any real power.

Augustus closely followed Caesar's
blueprint for the gladiatorial games.
He provided the Roman public with
"bread and circuses" like never before.
He handed out grain and money and built
grand new amphitheatres to hold the games.
Augustus's games would run for several
days in a row and feature thousands
of gladiators.

Augustus ordered that each game should follow the same daily schedule: animal hunts in the morning, public executions at lunchtime and gladiator fights in the afternoon. This schedule for the games would remain in place for the next 400 years.

Naval battle

For one of his gladiatorial games, Augustus ordered a large lake be built that could hold 30 ships. He then filled the lake with water and held a **naval** battle. Over 3,000 gladiators dressed as Roman **legionaries** then spent a day battling for the attending spectators.

3 WHO WERE THE GLADIATORS?

Gladiators were typically prisoners of wars, condemned criminals and enslaved people who had rebelled against Rome. Now, they would be forced to fight in front of a crowd. To do this they were trained at a gladiator school, called a *ludus*.

As Rome kept conquering new territories, thousands of prisoners of war were sent to a *ludus* to become gladiators. Because they had fought against Rome, these men were called *infamis*: the disgraced. They no longer had any rights. However, they had one chance to retrieve these rights. If they fought with bravery and honour in the amphitheatre, they might win back their freedom.

Little Rome

Under Augustus, Rome continued its policy of expansion. New territories were conquered and then turned into smaller versions of the city of Rome, with Roman baths, **aqueducts** for fresh water and amphitheatres for gladiatorial games. The newly conquered people would be free to live as citizens, as long as they didn't rebel. But those who did, would join the ranks of the *infamis*.

INSIDE THE LUDUS

Whatever life a gladiator trainee had come from, they would have to give it up when they entered the *ludus* gates. Inside, they would have to swear an oath agreeing "to endure to be burnt, to be bound, to be beaten, and to be killed by the sword". The punishment for not agreeing to this oath was execution. From now on, the gladiator was the property of the *ludus* owner.

On entering the *ludus*, each new recruit would be examined by a doctor to make sure they were fit for the many hours of rigorous training. The recruit would then be led into the central courtyard where the gladiators trained. Surrounding the yard were small buildings that included a kitchen and a mess (dining) hall, baths, an armoury, a prison for gladiators who tried to escape, a medical room, and the gladiators' cells.

Free gladiators

Some gladiators were free men who chose to fight. These men included Roman citizens, senators and even emperors. Some men became gladiators to avoid having to serve the normal 20 to 25 years of **military service**; others were ex-soldiers who couldn't adapt to **civilian** life. Some aristocratic Romans fought to regain lost honour, to make money, or just for the thrill of it.

A model of Rome's Ludus Maximus is shown here, with its central courtyard and surrounding buildings.

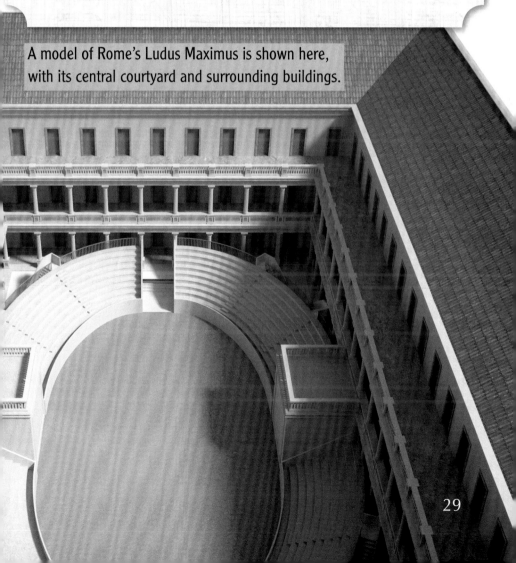

FOOD AND FIGHTING

A gladiator's day followed a strict routine. His cell would be unlocked at dawn and breakfast eaten in the mess hall. Then training would begin in the courtyard. New recruits would practise with a wooden sword, called a *rudis*. Gladiator training weapons were made large and heavy so the trainees could build up muscle. Their training was similar to that of Rome's legionaries.

Battle tactics

A *rudis* was based on the sword used by Roman legionaries. Legionaries used their swords to stab at opponents through the gaps in their **shield wall.**
Different formations formed out of shield walls was a central tactic used by the Roman army in battle. It was highly effective.

Gladiators would practise with their *rudis* against a two-metre-high pole.

Gladiator meals

Gladiators had the nickname *hordearii*, or "barley-porridge eaters", because of their diet. Gladiator porridge was a fatty, high-energy meal also fed to animals. It was designed to build up a level of fat around the gladiator's muscle to protect against sword cuts. Meat was only served the night before a fight. Often it would be from an animal hunted in the amphitheatre, such as a tiger or elephant.

FEES AND FUNERALS

After an initial period of training, a gladiator trainee would be assigned a gladiator type, depending on his physical build and ability. Each type fought with different armour and weapons and would be instructed by a specialist trainer. These trainers were ex-gladiators who had lived to tell the tale but were no longer fit to fight.

Gladiators in a *ludus* knew they might one day face each other in the arena. But despite this, close bonds formed. A group of gladiators would help the families of their fallen comrades and organise funerals. However, most gladiators only earned a small amount of money, so there was little to leave behind.

Gladiator money

It would cost between 1,000 and 15,000 *sestertii* to hire a gladiator to fight. (A loaf of bread in the late Republic cost around half a *sestertius*.) Most of the gladiator fee would go to the *ludus* owner, with the gladiator only receiving around 20%. Free men fighting as gladiators would get slightly more, often around 25%. However, a freed gladiator who returned to the amphitheatre to fight could collect a handsome fee.

4 SPARTACUS

There is little known about individual gladiators. Most were anonymous. They fought, died and are now forgotten. But the name of one gladiator lives on today: Spartacus. Spartacus was the gladiator leader who escaped captivity and raised an army against Rome.

Spartacus originally came from Thrace, a region covered by modern Bulgaria, Greece and Turkey.

BULGARIA

BLACK SEA

NORTHERN THRACE

EASTERN THRACE

WESTERN THRACE

SEA OF MARMARA

GREECE

AEGEAN SEA

TURKEY

Spartacus was a former Roman legionary who deserted from the army. He was then caught and enslaved. In 73 BCE, Spartacus was sold to a *ludus*, in Capua, Italy. The Capua *ludus* had a harsh reputation. Its gladiators were often beaten, underfed and locked in chains when not training. Spartacus and some of the gladiators plotted an escape.

One night, Spartacus and 70 gladiators stole kitchen knives, killed the *ludus* guards and escaped. As they made their way towards Mount Vesuvius, they came across a wagon carrying gladiator weapons. They attacked the wagon, armed themselves and set up camp on top of Mount Vesuvius.

Vesuvius and Pompeii

The volcano Mount Vesuvius famously erupted in 79 CE, burying the nearby cities of Pompeii and Herculaneum under metres of rock and ash. Centuries later, the cities were excavated and found to be nearly entirely intact.

GLADIATOR ARMY

When the Roman Senate heard about Spartacus, they sent an army to kill him. This army made camp at the bottom of Mount Vesuvius. But during the night, Spartacus and his gladiators climbed down the mountain on vines and killed the legionaries in their sleep. This meant Spartacus had now declared war on Rome.

News of Spartacus's victory quickly spread. Before long, tens of thousands of enslaved people escaped to join him. Spartacus taught them to fight like gladiators. Soon, this gladiator army was attacking Roman towns. As they did so, more enslaved people joined Spartacus.

Many people joining Spartacus had been enslaved by Rome their whole lives. Now, they had a chance to fight back.

Enslaved people in Rome

In ancient Rome, there were several ways to become enslaved. People could be captured in war or born into slavery. Others were enslaved as a punishment for crimes, or because of an unpaid debt. Enslaved people in Rome had no rights and could be treated in any way their owner saw fit. Many had to wear collars with their owner's address, like dogs. There were large markets in forums across the Roman Empire where you could buy an enslaved person. Most Roman families owned at least one enslaved person.

CLASHING ARMIES

By 72 CE, Spartacus's gladiators had won several battles against Rome's legionaries. The Senate then asked general Marcus Crassus to march 40,000 soldiers to meet Spartacus in battle. Spartacus had moved his camp to Southern Italy where he gathered more men. Now, he had an army capable of attacking the city of Rome.

Crassus and his army dug a ditch around Spartacus's camp to stop him escaping. But many of Crassus's men deserted. To make sure no one else deserted, Crassus executed one in every ten of his own men. These men were picked by lottery. Afterwards, Crassus ordered his army to attack Spartacus.

In the battle that followed, Spartacus tried to kill Crassus so that his army would fall apart. He nearly reached Crassus on the battlefield and managed to kill two of his bodyguards. But in the end, Spartacus was killed. The 6,000 survivors from Spartacus's army suffered an even more brutal fate. Every one of them was crucified. This means being nailed to a cross and left to die. Their crosses lined the road all the way to Rome, as a warning to others. There was never a gladiator **uprising** again.

Marcus Crassus was joined by general Pompey and his army at the end of Spartacus's rebellion.

39

5 THE EMPERORS' GAMES

After Augustus died in 14 CE, Rome was ruled by emperors. Armed with vast wealth and absolute power, these emperors created the most spectacular games Rome had ever seen. However, many of these emperors also had a well-founded reputation for being "bad, mad and dangerous". This meant they didn't have to answer to anyone and were free to behave as they wished.

Emperor Caligula loved the gladiatorial games and, at first, he was loved by the Roman people. He spent vast sums on his games and gave spectators meat and other gifts. But before long, Caligula's behaviour became bizarre and unpredictable.

Caligula was going bald and hated men with hair. He would order they shave their heads into ridiculous styles. Sometimes, he ordered the sails that gave spectators shade to be pulled back, so they would bake in the hot sun. Caligula then began appearing in the arena as a gladiator. Many Romans found this disgraceful.

In the end, Caligula's behaviour led to his downfall. This happened when he announced he would elect his horse as Consul. The horse had a jewelled collar and its own palace to live in. After his announcement, Caligula was **assassinated** by the Praetorian Guard. Few Romans, however, were sad to see Caligula go.

The Praetorian Guard

The Praetorian Guard was an elite unit of soldiers charged with protecting the emperor. However, the guard was often corrupt. They would sometimes decide to assassinate an emperor and at other times could be bribed to do so.

EMPEROR CLAUDIUS

After Caligula was assassinated, Claudius was made emperor. Claudius set about creating gladiatorial games that he said "no one had ever seen, or would see again". These ran for several days in a row and included entirely new events.

Claudius loved the games and introduced animal hunts to the Circus Maximus, as well as amphitheatres. Here, panthers and bulls would be hunted down by the Praetorian Guard. Claudius would also participate in the games himself, by entering the arena and giving victorious gladiators gifts of gold. He was also known for granting gladiators their freedom if the crowd pleaded with him to do so.

One of Claudius's most spectacular events was a sea battle staged on a lake. Over 19,000 condemned criminals were trained to fight in the battle as gladiators. They greeted Claudius with the words, "We who are about to die salute you", a line later made famous in gladiator movies.

EMPEROR NERO

Claudius kept the Roman people happy with his large number of games. But he was not so smart in his personal life. He married his niece Agrippina, who helped him rule. But Agrippina had her own ambitions. In 54 CE, it was suspected that she murdered Claudius with a poisoned plate of mushrooms. She then asked the Praetorian Guard to install her son Nero as emperor.

Emperor Nero put on gladiatorial games with a twist. These games included senators and convicted criminals appearing as gladiators and also fighting animals. Fights between female gladiators were also organised. However, Nero ordered that no one could be killed during these games. Instead, he pleased the crowd by giving out grain, jewels, enslaved people, apartments, ships and farms.

Like Caligula, Nero's behaviour became increasingly bizarre. He began appearing on stage as an actor and a gladiator about to be killed, which was considered disgraceful for an emperor. He then executed several Roman senators and even his own mother, Agrippina. Most Romans soon realised that Nero was dangerous. In the end, the Praetorian Guard made him an enemy of the state. Nero then committed suicide before he could be assassinated. His death was celebrated in Rome.

6 TYPES OF GLADIATOR

ARMOUR AND WEAPONS

Different gladiator types had different armour and weapons.
But most used a helmet, sword, shield and leg greaves.
A treasure trove of these items was found in pristine
condition during the excavation of Pompeii.

HELMETS

A helmet gave a gladiator his striking and
sometimes sinister appearance. Made from
copper and iron, helmets often featured
a visor, eye holes and a crest on top.
The inside of the helmet was padded
for extra protection and comfort.

SWORDS

The gladiator's sword was a double-
bladed steel sword 65 centimetres long.
Later, it was shortened to 50 centimetres.

SHIELD

A gladiator's rectangular shield was made from three layers of wood, with an outer layer of leather and a bronze dome on the front. A smaller round shield was made from one piece of bronze.

GREAVES

Greaves were a gladiator's shin guards. Greaves were made from one sheet of beaten bronze and were sometimes strapped over leg wrappings for extra protection.

the amphitheatre at Pompeii

There were several different gladiator types.
Many were based on enemy warriors defeated by Rome.
By showcasing the weapons and armour of these warriors
in the arena, the public were reminded of Rome's victories.
Each gladiator type would be pitted against another type
who would give a good contest.

THRAEX

One of the earliest
gladiator types,
the *thraex* was based
on Thracian warriors.
The *thraex* was easy
to spot because of his
plumed helmet with
a crest in the shape of
the mythological **griffin**.

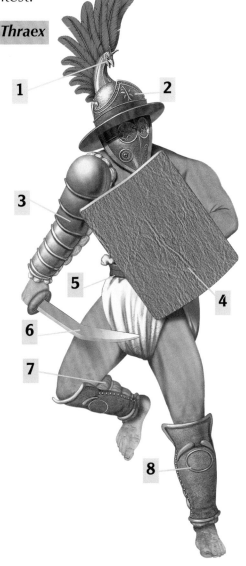

Thraex

1 griffin crest
2 brimmed helmet with plumes
3 armour on one arm
4 small rectangular shield
5 loin cloth and belt
6 short, curved sword
7 padded wrapping around legs
8 leg greaves

HOPLOMACHUS

The *hoplomachus* was a popular gladiator modelled on ancient Greek soldiers, the **hoplites**. Like all gladiator types, the *hoplomachus* fought a specific opponent in the arena. For the *hoplomachus*, this often meant fighting against the similarly-armed *thraex*.

Hoplomachus

1 visored helmet

2 spear

3 small, round bronze shield

4 long dagger

5 leg greaves

6 padded leg wrappings or quilted trousers

RETIARIUS AND SECUTOR

Two of the most famous gladiator types were the *retiarius* and *secutor*. They were designed to fight against each other, but they had different armour and weapons. Unlike many other gladiator types, the *retiarius* and *secutor* weren't based on enemy warriors.

RETIARIUS

Inspired by the sea, the *retiarius* fought by throwing his net to ensnare his opponent. But once his net was thrown, the *retiarius* had only a **trident** and dagger to fight with. The *retiarius* had little armour, so would try not to get within an opponent's stabbing range.

Retiarius

1 metal guard on shoulder

2 1.8 metre-long trident

3 short dagger

4 net

50

SECUTOR

If a *retiarius* looked like a fisherman, then the *secutor* was the fish he was trying to catch. The *secutor's* fish-shaped helmet was smooth to avoid being ensnared by a net. Its eyeholes were too small for trident points to penetrate. This also made it hot inside and difficult to see. However, the *secutor* and *retiarius* were considered an excellent match.

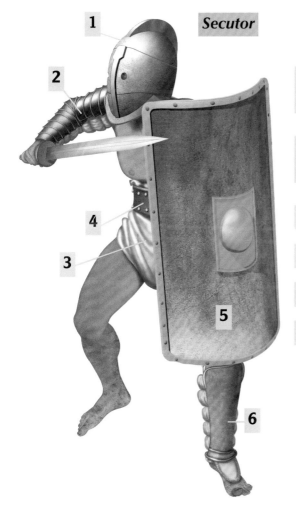

Secutor

1 helmet with small eyeholes and fin-shaped crest

2 leather wrapping on right arm

3 loincloth

4 wide, leather belt

5 rectangular shield

6 one leg greave

PROVOCATOR

The *provocator* was a type of gladiator partly modelled on Roman legionaries who fought in Gaul. A medium-armed gladiator, the *provocator* was the only one to wear breastplate armour. He would only fight against another *provocator*.

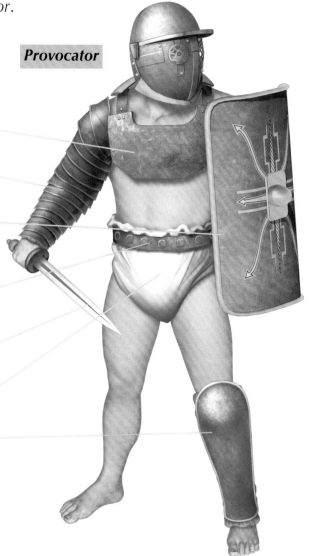

Provocator

metal breastplate

armour on one arm

medium-sized
rectangular shield

broad metal belt

short sword

heavy loincloth

one leg greave

PROVOCATOR VS PROVOCATOR

The *provocator* fought barefoot, which allowed quick, darting movements and lightning-fast counter-attacks. His shield was used to knock an opponent off his feet and hide behind between attacks. A *provocator*'s helmet reached down to protect his neck, but was heavy and stuffy, with only small holes to see through. Within minutes, the gladiator's head would be running with sweat. The short sword would be used for stabbing thrusts. A *provocator* contest would be fast, furious and often over quickly.

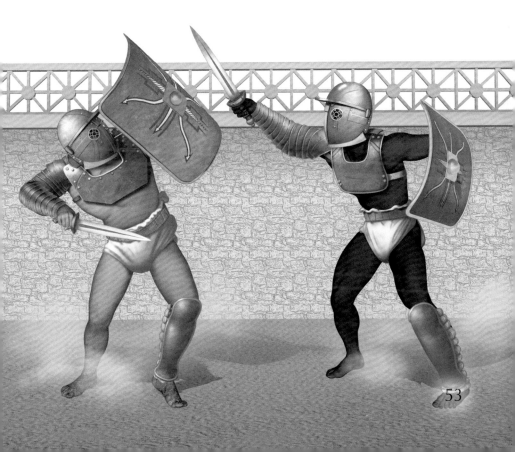

7 THE COLOSSEUM

The Colosseum was the greatest gladiator amphitheatre ever constructed. Built to seat over 50,000 spectators, the Colosseum had two purposes in mind. It was designed to help people forget Emperor Nero, and also to bring vast and varied forms of violent entertainment to the Roman people.

Rome was in bad shape after Nero. He had nearly bankrupted the empire with his extravagant spending and, in 64 CE, a fire had devastated the city. In 70 CE, new Emperor Vespasian announced plans for a huge amphitheatre as

The Colosseum took its name from the "Colossus" statue of Nero, which stood nearby.

a gift to the public. It was hoped this *Amphitheatrum Flavium* – nicknamed the Colosseum – would act as a type of rebirth for the city. However, it was such an ambitious project that it took eight years to complete.

The Colosseum was built by tens of thousands of enslaved people captured in Jerusalem. To start the building, the enslaved people had to drain a lake, excavate over 30,000 tonnes of earth, and lay 12-metre-high foundations. They then constructed the 50-metre-high Colosseum from over 100,000 tonnes of rock, 300 tonnes of iron and thousands of tonnes of marble. The end result was a marvel of arches, columns, steps, statues and seating.

the Colosseum today

INSIDE THE COLOSSEUM

When finished, the Colosseum was a state-of-the-art amphitheatre designed to keep the crowd constantly entertained and comfortable. This meant providing new and novel events to prevent boredom, as well as large sails for shade and sprays of water to keep spectators cool.

A thick layer of sand covered the wooden arena floor.

The *hypogeum* was the space below the arena floor. It was an underground labyrinth of cells, tunnels and cages

The Hypogeum

The *hypogeum* was like a giant backstage area.
Here, props, animals and people to be executed were kept before making their entrance. Then, a series of pulleys, lifts and trapdoors would bring them into the arena as if by magic. This system also meant whole sets of trees and bushes could be brought up for the animal hunts.

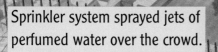

Sprinkler system sprayed jets of perfumed water over the crowd.

large sails suspended on long poles to provide shade

Seating was divided by class and rank. The senators and emperor sat closest to the arena floor.

The imperial box is where the emperor sat.

The highest tier of seating was for women and foreign visitors.

the gladiators' gateway, where the gladiators entered to parade themselves and fight

Statues of emperors and gods were placed in archways around the outer walls.

57

8 COMMODUS

No other Roman emperor loved the gladiatorial games like Commodus. He held numerous games and often appeared in the Colosseum himself as a gladiator. He even called himself "one of the greatest gladiators who ever lived". His fights, however, were almost always staged.

Commodus became Roman Emperor in 180 CE, after his father Marcus Aurelius died. Aurelius was known as the last of the "Five Good Emperors". Commodus, by contrast, was a bad emperor, just like Caligula, Claudius and Nero, who had gone before him.

Commodus used to accuse innocent wealthy Roman aristocrats of committing crimes and would then demand money to drop the charges. Other aristocrats were simply killed for their fortunes. Commodus then used the money to spoil himself and pay for his lavish lifestyle. The money also helped stage large, gladiatorial games. For this, the Roman public loved Commodus; at least, to begin with.

As emperor, Commodus ordered the head on Nero's Colossus statue be replaced with one showing him.

Cassius Dio

Cassius Dio, a senator and historian during Commodus's rule, was one of the emperor's main critics. Dio said Commodus was responsible for turning Rome "from a kingdom of gold to one of rust and iron". Many modern historians think the decline of the Roman Empire began with Commodus.

HUNTING HERCULES

Commodus used to dress in lion skin, carry a club and liken himself to the mythical character Hercules. On the day of the games, Commodus would have his Hercules outfit carried before him on a cushion. He would then undergo several costume changes in his imperial box, changing from a white silk toga and gold crown to a simple tunic. He would then enter the arena barefoot to announce the morning animal hunts.

Commodus would join the animal hunts by firing arrows and spears from the imperial box. Once he killed 100 bears in this way. He would then drink from a cup shaped like a club, while the spectators called out, "Long life to you."

An athletic man with fair hair and a beard, Commodus often dressed as Hercules.

In the afternoon, Commodus introduced the gladiator fights. He would often appear himself, dressed as a *secutor*. However, his fights were not real. Commodus fought with a wooden *rudis* and would always win, as no opponent would dare defeat the emperor. However, Commodus would pay himself up to one million sestertii for winning. This was a colossal amount of money, especially for a gladiator.

END OF COMMODUS

After his gladiator bout, Commodus would dress as the god Mercury and retire to the imperial box. From here, he would watch the real gladiator fights, while shouting commands and encouraging gladiators to be increasingly violent. He would typically order gladiators to kill their defeated opponents, rather than spare them.

Over time, people became scared of Commodus. Many stayed away from the Colosseum after a rumour spread that Commodus was going to shoot spectators with a bow and arrow. On another occasion, during the animal hunts, Commodus beheaded an ostrich and walked towards the attending senators. One of the senators was Cassius Dio, who wrote that Commodus "wagged his head with a grin, indicating that he would treat us in the same way". However, instead of being scared, Dio said the senators chewed laurel leaves so Commodus couldn't see them laughing.

Commodus's end came when he announced he would begin the year 193 CE from a gladiator *ludus* cell while dressed as a *secutor*. When his mistress Marcia tried to talk him out of the plan, Commodus ordered her to be executed. But Marcia discovered the plot and ordered the Praetorian Guard to help her. The guard hired a wrestler to kill Commodus. Thus ended the life of the gladiator emperor.

9 BEING A GLADIATOR

Gladiators weren't always men – women too sometimes fought in the arena. Female gladiators were usually enslaved people or prisoners forced to fight. But free and even aristocratic women also appeared as gladiators. Some emperors, however, tried to ban the practice of female gladiators.

Many Romans didn't believe women should be gladiators. To please these people, Emperor Augustus forbade any woman under 20 years old from appearing in the arena. Emperor Tiberius ruled that no aristocratic woman should be a gladiator. Emperor Nero, however, used not only female gladiators in his games, but female animal hunters as well.

Not all emperors encouraged female gladiators.
In 200 CE, the practice was banned completely.

Achillea and Amazonia

Two of the most famous female gladiators were
Achillea and Amazonia. A marble **relief** showing
the pair fighting was found in modern-day Turkey.
The gladiators are shown wearing loincloths instead
of tunics and are armed with swords, large shields,
leg greaves and arm protectors. Their helmets
have been thrown to one side, perhaps to show
the audience that they were not men. However, little
else is known about Achillea and Amazonia.

AFTER THE ARENA

For most gladiators, there were only three ways out of
the arena: victory, death, or being given a reprieve by
the emperor. A reprieve meant a gladiator could fight
another day. Those gladiators who had fought especially
well, however, might be granted their freedom.

Gladiators were only set free on occasion, but it was a great
crowd-pleaser when it happened. To do this, the emperor
would present the gladiator with a wooden *rudis* as
a symbol of their freedom. To great applause, the gladiator
would then walk out of the arena a free man. However, few
freed gladiators had made enough money to retire. Instead,
they would have to find work in the outside world.

Employment for ex-gladiators was limited. Some worked as bodyguards for rich aristocrats. Others opened bars or restaurants. Because the gladiator was famous, he would attract customers – at least for a while. Others chose to return to the world of gladiators as a trainer. An ex-gladiator who became a trainer was good for a *ludus* owner – it showed gladiator trainees that it was possible to survive. Some even decided to fight in the arena once more.

Roman bar

FAMOUS GLADIATORS

It may seem odd that a freed gladiator would think of risking life and limb to fight again. But returning gladiators were often offered high fees to return for one last fight. Emperor Tiberius once tempted one such gladiator with a purse of 100,000 sestertii. This was a small fortune for any Roman.

Nero was known to reward victorious gladiators handsomely. He gave one called Spiculus several properties.

FLAMMA

A famous returning gladiator was called Flamma. Flamma was granted his freedom four times, but he kept choosing to come back to the arena and fight. His gravestone in Sicily has the following inscription:

"Flamma, secutor, lived 30 years, fought 34 times, won 21 times, fought to a draw nine times, defeated four times, a Syrian by nationality ..."

Disgraced celebrity

Famous gladiators were like the rock stars of the ancient world. People gossiped about them, went to the *ludus* to get a glimpse of them training and could sometimes pay to visit their cell. But even famous gladiators who won their freedom would never have the same rights as a Roman citizen. Instead, they would always be considered *infamis*, or the disgraced, according to the rules of Roman society.

FIGHTING ODDS

Little is known about a gladiator's chances of survival in the arena. However, tomb inscriptions and gladiator advertising show us that gladiators didn't always have to win a fight to come away with their lives.

An ancient tomb inscription describes one gladiator who had survived 30 bouts in the arena, despite only winning half of them. This means the gladiator was often given a reprieve, rather than being killed. Another inscription records a man losing his life at the age of 21, after five fights and four years in a *ludus*. A different inscription reports a gladiator retired after 20 years and 19 victories, who later died a free man at 48 years old.

There are no recorded odds for gladiators, but their chance of survival increased with experience. However, some writers report that the average gladiator was killed within the first two years of their five-year contract. Gladiators were usually expected to fight at two or three games a year, although there are records of one gladiator fighting every day for nine days in a row at Emperor Trajan's games. He was then granted his freedom by the emperor.

10 THE DEMISE OF THE GAMES

The gladiatorial games were designed to show off the might and majesty of the Roman Empire. But by the late 3rd century, the empire fell under increasing attack from various peoples, including the Germanic civilisation, and its borders shrank. The games too, began their slow demise.

Many emperors came and went during the end of the Roman Empire. Forty-nine emperors alone were enthroned between 239 and 285 CE. One of the last great emperors was Constantine. But Constantine didn't approve of the games. He banned gladiator fights in 313 CE. Despite this, gladiator fights still occurred until 440 CE. But by then, there was little money to be spent on the games. The public's appetite, too, seems to have waned. In 476 CE, the last Western Roman Emperor, Romulus Augustulus, was overthrown by the Germanic prince Odovacar. Odovacar then became king of Italy, marking the end of the Western Roman Empire.

After the collapse of the Roman Empire, the Colosseum fell into disrepair. For over 1000 years, it crumbled into ruin. However, from 1874, archaeologists began to restore the Colosseum. Today, it's a popular tourist site.

Odovacar accepting the surrender of Romulus Augustulus.

CONCLUSION

It has been over 1,500 years since the last known gladiatorial games were held. Today, it's hard to imagine this violent spectacle was popular entertainment, enjoyed by many. And yet, the games continue to fascinate us. Today, millions of tourists visit the Colosseum every year.

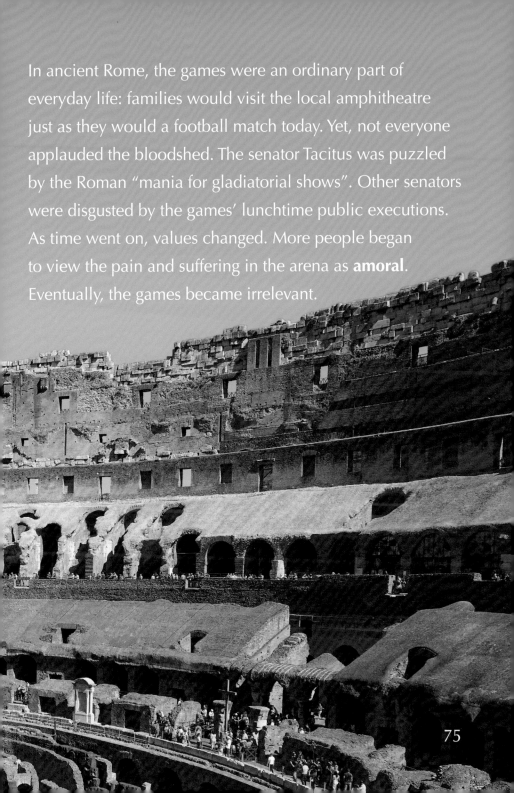

In ancient Rome, the games were an ordinary part of everyday life: families would visit the local amphitheatre just as they would a football match today. Yet, not everyone applauded the bloodshed. The senator Tacitus was puzzled by the Roman "mania for gladiatorial shows". Other senators were disgusted by the games' lunchtime public executions. As time went on, values changed. More people began to view the pain and suffering in the arena as **amoral**. Eventually, the games became irrelevant.

GLOSSARY

amoral morally incorrect behaviour

amphitheatre a round or oval-shaped building where gladiator games were held

aqueducts human-made channels for carrying water

arena the sandy floor in the middle of an amphitheatre

aristocrats people of noble birth

assassinated murdered an important person

blueprint a plan of action

civilian non-soldier

civil war a war between people in the same country

Consul a chief official of Rome, two of which were elected every year

democracy a government elected by the people

dictator a person who has been granted unlimited power

empire a vast set of lands ruled over by an emperor

griffin a mythical creature with the head of an eagle and body of a lion

heir next in line to someone after they die

hoplites heavily-armed ancient Greek soldiers

legionaries ancient Roman soldiers

military service a necessary period in the army, required by law

naval relating to ships

oath a promise to do something

relief a work of art that is raised, often on a wall

republic ruled by a government, rather than a monarch or emperor

Senate the supreme council of ancient Rome, made up of senators

shield wall a defensive army formation made up of overlapping shields

submit to acknowledge defeat

trident a three-pronged spear

tyrant a person who rules harshly and without limits

uprising when people get together to rebel in protest against people in power

INDEX

EMPERORS AND GLADIATORS THROUGH TIME

Name: Spartacus
Rank: Gladiator
Fate: Killed in battle

Name: Claudius
Rank: Emperor
Fate: Poisoned

150 BCE   100 BCE   50 BCE   0   50 CE   100 CE   150 CE

Names: Achillea and Amazonia
Rank: Gladiators
Fate: Unknown

Name: Caligula
Rank: Emperor
Fate: Assassinated

Name: Commodus
Rank: Emperor
Fate: Assassinated

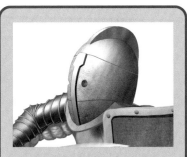

Name: Flamma
Rank: Gladiator
Fate: Unknown

250 CE   300 CE   350 CE   400 CE   450 CE   500 CE   550 CE

Name: Nero
Rank: Emperor
Fate: Suicide

Name: Romulus Augustulus
Rank: Western Roman Emperor
Fate: Unknown

79

Ideas for reading

Written by Gill Matthews
Primary Literacy Consultant

Reading objectives:

- check that the book makes sense to them, discussing their understanding and exploring the meaning of words in context
- summarise the main ideas drawn from more than one paragraph, identifying key details that support the main ideas
- retrieve, record and present information from non-fiction
- explain and discuss their understanding of what they have read, including through formal presentations and debates, maintaining a focus on the topic and using notes where necessary

Spoken language objectives:

- use relevant strategies to build their vocabulary
- articulate and justify answers, arguments and opinions
- use spoken language to develop understanding through speculating, hypothesising, imagining and exploring ideas
- participate in discussions, presentations, performances, role play, improvisations and debates

Curriculum links: History – The Roman Empire and its impact on Britain

Interest words: fascinate, applauded, puzzled, disgusted

Build a context for reading

- Ask children to explore the covers. Ask what they think emperors and gladiators might be.
- Encourage children to tell you what they know about Roman times.
- Ask what they think they will find out from the book.
- Discuss the features that information books have. Give children time to skim the book to find the contents, glossary and index. Establish the purpose and organisation of these features.

Understand and apply reading strategies

- Read pp2–3 aloud. Ask children to explain what emperors and gladiators are.